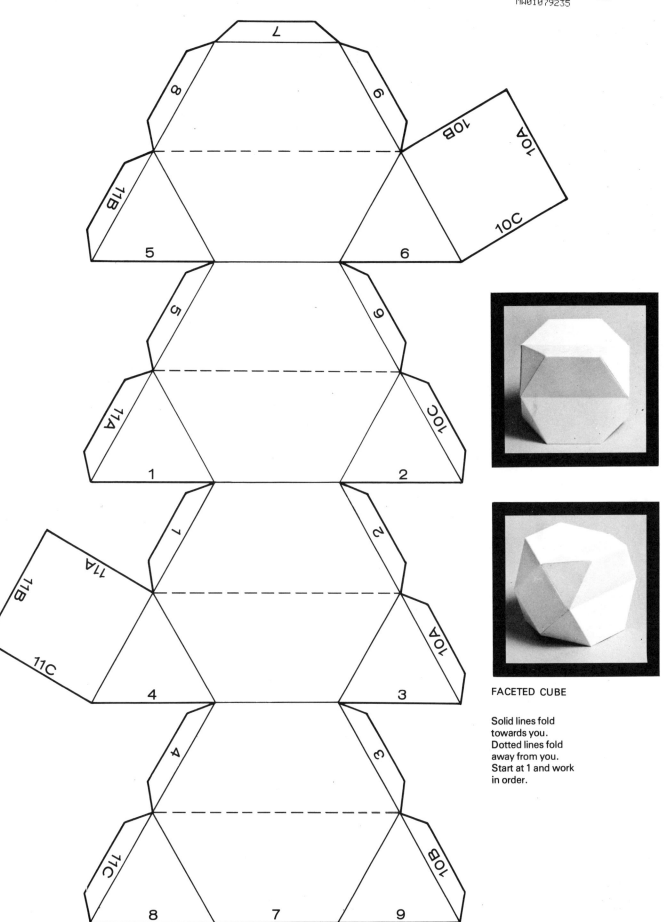

FACETED CUBE

Solid lines fold
towards you.
Dotted lines fold
away from you.
Start at 1 and work
in order.

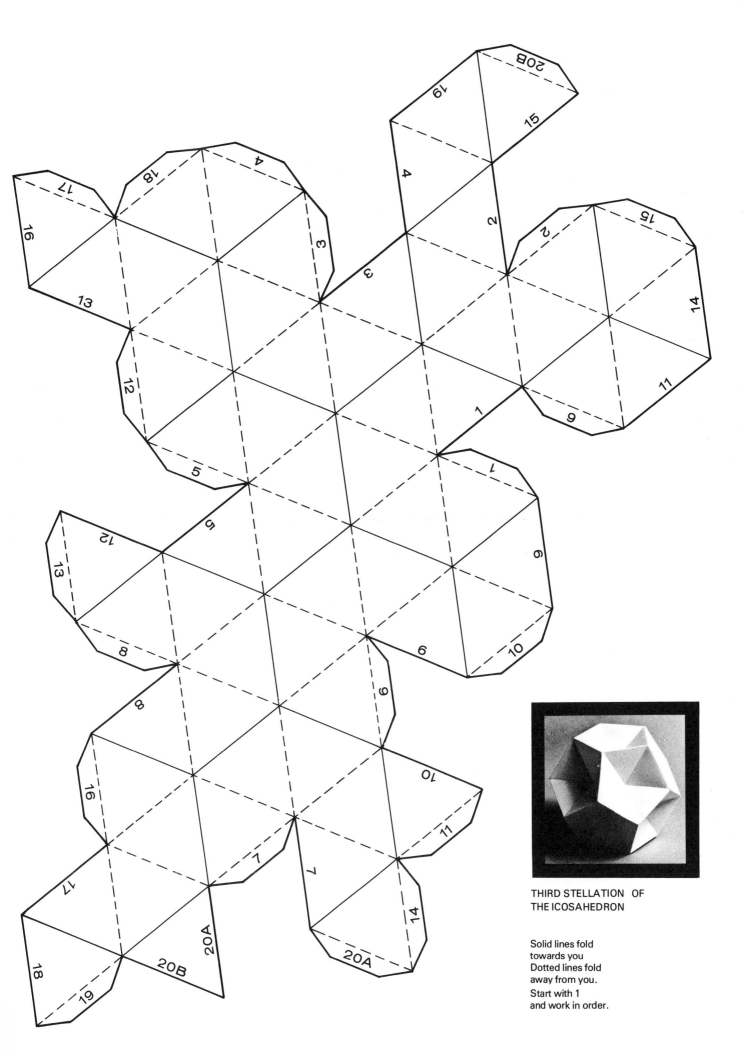

THIRD STELLATION OF
THE ICOSAHEDRON

Solid lines fold
towards you
Dotted lines fold
away from you.
Start with 1
and work in order.

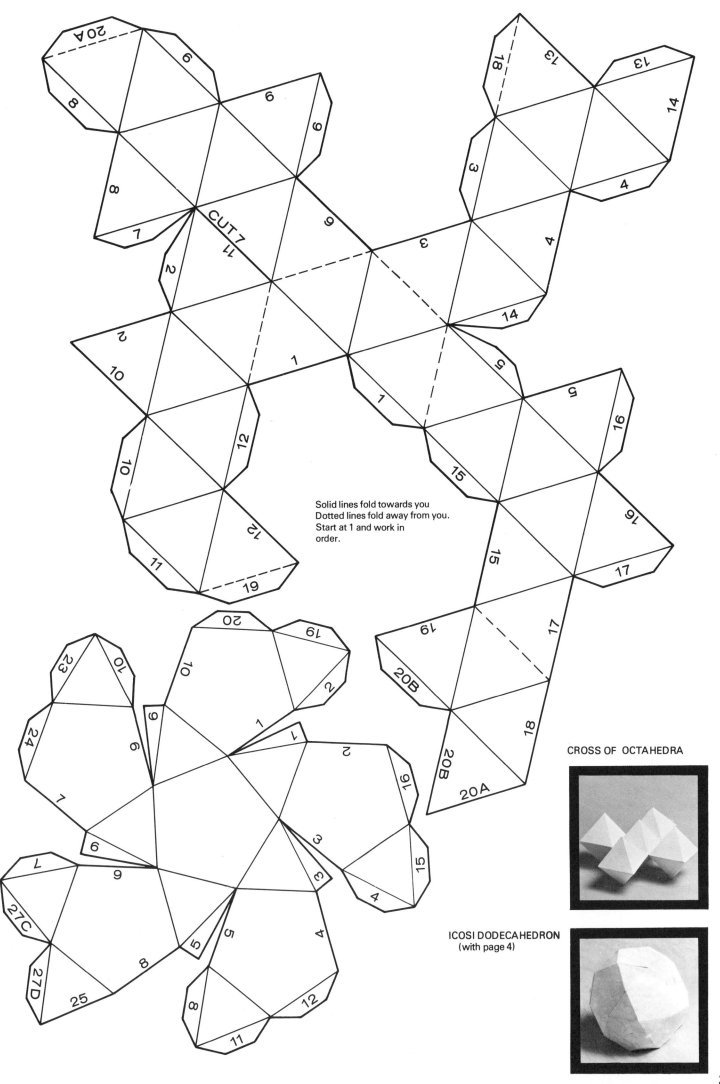

Solid lines fold towards you
Dotted lines fold away from you.
Start at 1 and work in
order.

CUT 7

CROSS OF OCTAHEDRA

ICOSI DODECAHEDRON
(with page 4)

3

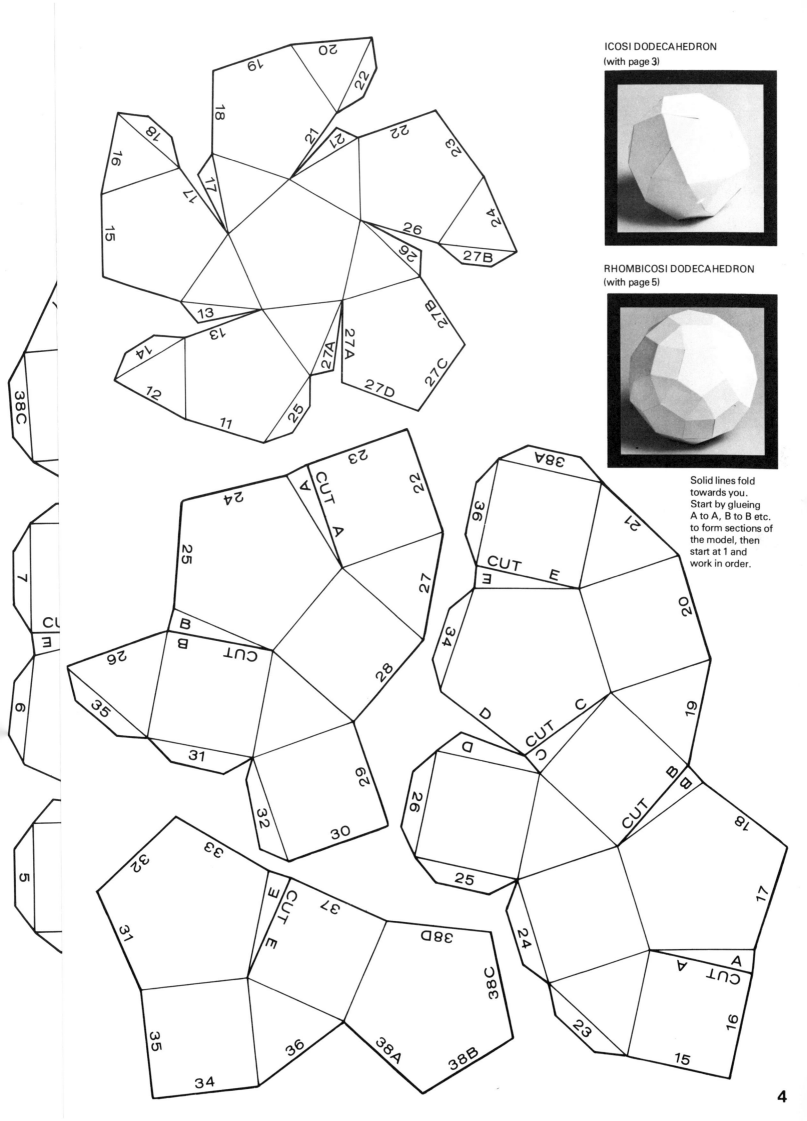

ICOSI DODECAHEDRON
(with page 3)

RHOMBICOSI DODECAHEDRON
(with page 5)

Solid lines fold
towards you.
Start by glueing
A to A, B to B etc.
to form sections of
the model, then
start at 1 and
work in order.

4

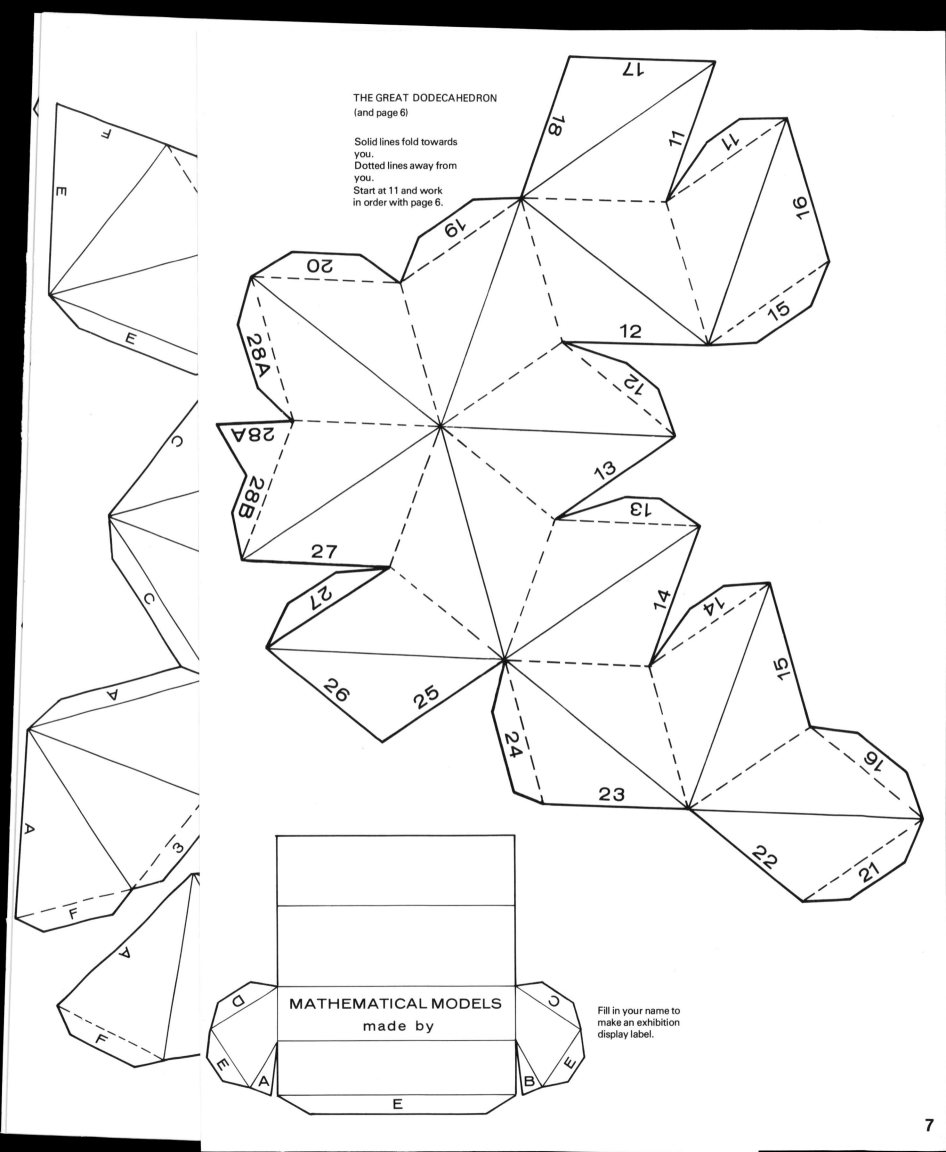

THE GREAT DODECAHEDRON
(and page 6)

Solid lines fold towards
you.
Dotted lines away from
you.
Start at 11 and work
in order with page 6.

MATHEMATICAL MODELS

made by

Fill in your name to
make an exhibition
display label.

7

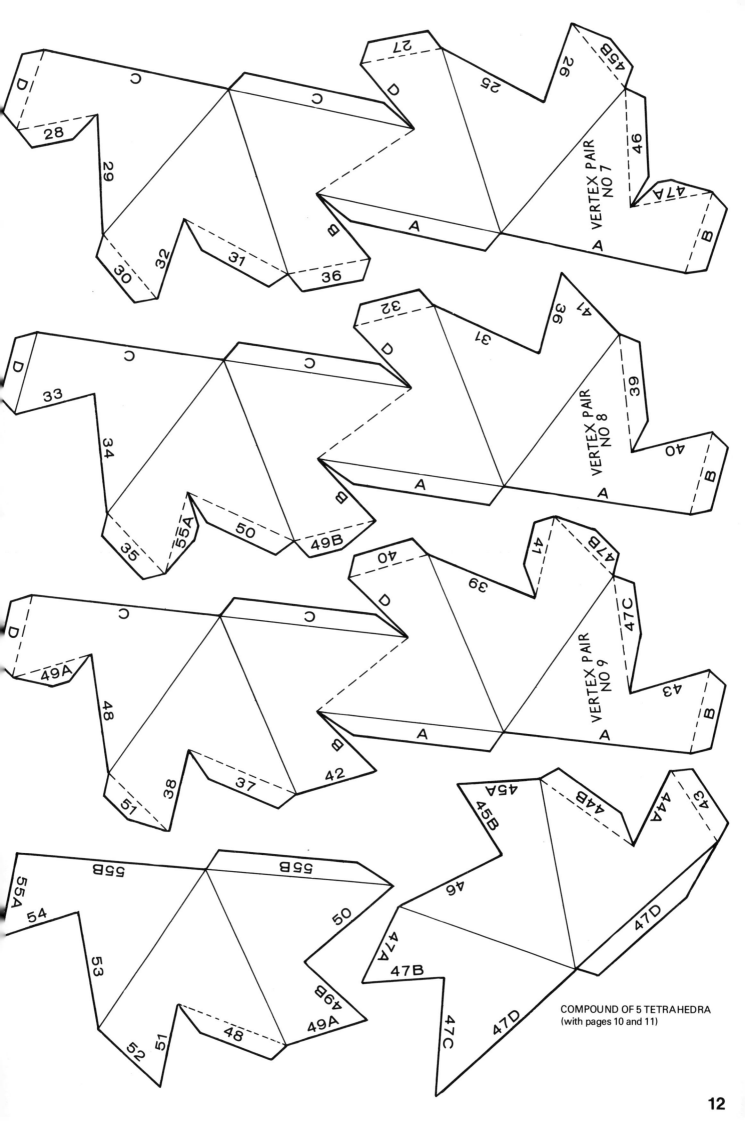

VERTEX PAIR NO 7

VERTEX PAIR NO 8

VERTEX PAIR NO 9

COMPOUND OF 5 TETRAHEDRA
(with pages 10 and 11)